CONTENTS

This booklet has been inspired by the struggles and triumphs of the many separated families we have had the privilege to work with over the years. We would like to acknowledge their contribution to the ideas in these chapters. We are particularly grateful to Sheena Connolly, Avril Tobin, Adrienne Fox and the many other parents who commented on the manuscript, and also to our colleagues in the Mater Hospital. We also acknowledge the contribution of Peter Reid from the Lucena Clinic in the writing of the first edition.

PARENTAL SEPARATION

INTRODUCTION

Separation and divorce are on the increase. More and more children are witnessing their parents separate and/or growing up in single parent households. The chain of events from parental conflict to separation and divorce can have a devastating impact on parents, children and extended families. In surveys, parental separation is second only to the death of a parent in the levels of stress it can cause in children and parents. In addition, separation can bring many other stressful events to bear, such as house moves, money problems, legal battles and loss of supportive relationships, all of which can increase the burden on parents and children.

THE PURPOSE OF THIS BOOKLET

The purpose of this booklet is to help parents help themselves and their children to cope better with separation and divorce. The booklet includes practical advice and suggestions that are based on extensive research into what makes a difference for children coming to terms with their parents' separation.

WE NEED TO CUT DOWN STRESS ON OUR KIDS BY MINIMISING THE CHANGES IN THEIR LIVES...

YOU'RE RIGHT— AND AT LEAST THE FACT THAT WE LOVE THEM HASN'T CHANGED.

THE GOOD NEWS

The good news is that there are positive things you can do that will minimise the negative impact of separation on your children. According to research studies, children can suffer a range of emotional and social difficulties on account of their parents' separation. A significant number of children cope relatively well, however, and this booklet will help to point you in that direction.

Their coping positively largely depends on *how their parents manage the separation*. To achieve this, it is essential that as parents you make some headway towards achieving the following goals.

- Take steps to manage your own stress to ensure you personally are coping.

- Listen to your children and focus on their best interests and needs.

- Work constructively with your former partner on parenting issues.

- Maintain the quality of your own parenting.

- Minimise the changes in your child's life after the separation.

If you can do these things, then you are doing a lot to help your children manage the separation, and you are taking steps towards a more harmonious living environment. This booklet aims to build on what you are already doing right and to further improve your own and your children's coping.

ACHIEVING SHARED PARENTING

Throughout this booklet we emphasise the importance of achieving shared parenting after the separation. Though there are exceptions (e.g. in cases of violence or abuse), shared parenting is generally the best situation for most children post separation. Shared parenting gives children access to the care, support and love of their two parents, working together for the benefit of their children. These are the ideal conditions in which children can thrive and grow up as well-adjusted adults.

We also recognise, however, that this ideal is far from easy; in reality, many parents find themselves either as single parents coping relatively on their own with their children, or as 'live-away' parents struggling to stay supportively involved in their children's lives. Though the situation is changing (as more fathers have an active role in childcare before and after separation), the ideal of shared parenting is still relatively rare. The most common situation is for the children to live with one parent (usually the mother) and then have weekly or less

CAN WE STILL FIND THINGS TO LIKE ABOUT EACH OTHER?

OF COURSE WE CAN — I LIKE HOW WE'RE BOTH TRYING TO DO RIGHT BY OUR CHILDREN ...

frequent access with the other parent (usually the father). For this reason, we have included two chapters that focus on the respective experiences and challenges of being a single and a live-away parent. As a parent reading these chapters you may find yourself identifying with either or both perspectives. Indeed the roles are often interchangeable, and you may have the dual experience of being both a single parent when the children are with you and of being a live-away parent when they are with your former partner.

THE AUTHORS

The two of us work in child and adolescent mental health services. In writing this book we bring together our professional experience of working with hundreds of separated families, and one of us (Eugene) also brings his experience of being a separated father. As two male authors, we consulted widely with separated mothers to try and ensure their perspective is included in the book, and we hope the book is of benefit to all separated mothers and fathers whatever their circumstances.

COPING AS A PARENT

THE EFFECT OF SEPARATION ON PARENTS

Parental conflict leading to separation and/or divorce is hugely stressful for parents. The turmoil and devastation can last a long time. It can be a long arduous journey lasting many years, starting with the awareness of difficulties in your relationship to the final decision to separate and then on to the path of developing stable separate living arrangements for you and your children.

Before the decision to separate there may be a long period of uncertainty and upset, of breaks and reconciliations, and often very open conflict. After the separation there can be a long period of instability as lifestyles and living arrangements are thrown into turmoil.

It is not surprising that during this period you may feel you are really in for a rough ride. You can feel depressed, deeply hurt, guilty, angry, outraged, even suicidal and homicidal. You may feel your whole world has  caved in, that your dreams are shattered, and feel a failure that you haven't made your relationship or marriage work.

You can also be acutely aware of the distress of your children and be plagued by guilt about this. In addition, there can be great stigma and shame associated with being separated. Whereas with a terrible event like bereavement you can be guaranteed the support of your family and friends, sometimes there is less support when you have separated. People are often looking for 'whose fault it is' and 'someone to blame' and this can add to the burden.

When parents separate, they are usually at very different stages in the process. Rarely do both parties arrive at the decision at the same time. One parent is usually unhappy and upset in the relationship or marriage for a long time and then initiates the separation. This parent can go through great upset and guilt at ending the relationship and because of the hurt caused to the children and their former partner. The other parent is liable to feel shock and devastation. They can feel deeply hurt, guilty and wounded as they come to terms with the fact that the relationship is finally over. Though parents start out at different stages, over time they tend to move through the whole range of feelings. Whether they initiated the separation or not, both parents can swing between feeling hurt and victimised by the other to feeling very guilty at causing the relationship or marriage to end.

As well as the negative feelings associated with parental separation, there can also be feelings of relief and new hope. This is especially the case if the relationship has been conflictual and unhappy for some time or indeed if it has been abusive. The separation can be the end of a long process and signify an opportunity for parents to begin to put their difficulties behind them and to start life again.

Whatever point you are at in the separation process, be prepared for a roller-coaster of emotions and a difficult and challenging time for yourself and your children. The best place to start is where you are right now.

LEARNING TO COPE AS A PARENT

Though it takes time, courage and great compassion, parents do cope with separation and divorce. Some parents may get stuck in resentment, ongoing conflict and disputes, but many parents find the resources to move on, work out a constructive relationship with their former partner, and rebuild their lives for themselves and their children. For your children's sake it is absolutely essential that you do take steps to cope as soon as possible. Whatever their ages, children can suffer greatly on account of their parents' separation. This is especially the case when there is on-going conflict and bitterness and/or when parents are caught up in their own preoccupations and unable to attend to their children's needs. Children can suffer greatly during parental conflict, separation and divorce and *need the support and care of both their parents more than ever.*

This can be hard to do if you are weakened and drained emotionally and mentally by your own experience of the separation. Your children, however, need you during this period. Even though you feel at your weakest, you are called on to be at your strongest. Remember you are your child's greatest asset during this difficult time. For this reason you need to take steps to care for yourself and to cope personally, not only for yourself but also for the sake of your children.

So what can you do to help yourself cope during this difficult time?

- *Take care of yourself and ensure you get support.*

Don't go through this period alone. Make sure you meet and talk to people who you feel can understand and support you. Find friends and family members who can support you emotionally. Remember that extended family members such as grandparents, or close friends, may have their own grief about the end of your relationship or may have a biased view and may not be able to fully support you. If this is the case, try and find people who have some distance from the situation and who can give you a more balanced view. This might mean making contact with old friends and asking for the support you need. If it's helpful, seek out support groups or meetings for separating and separated parents. There are also many counselling services, both general and specific to separating parents, that could be invaluable to you. You will find a list of services at the back of this booklet.

- *Give yourself time.*

Remember that coping with separation is a long process and can be cyclical. There will be bad times when you feel low or upset, but remember that these will pass and things will get easier in the long term. Try and maintain an optimistic outlook, focusing on the practical things you can do rather than worrying excessively.

- *Practice self care and relaxation.*

Parents under stress often stop eating well or exercising or doing things they enjoy. This can cause even greater stress. This is the time when you really do need to look after yourself, by ensuring you eat well, exercise, get good rest and relaxation and maintain some enjoyable outlets. The more energised and refreshed you can be the more available you can be for your children.

- *Begin the healing process.*

All things being equal, the hardest thing for parents can be to forgive themselves or their former partner for what has happened and to let go of excessive resentment, hurt and guilt. These strong negative emotions, however, can be damaging. Resentment about your former partner can limit your ability to co-parent and can be indirectly communicated to your children, making it 'not OK' for them to love their other parent. Excessive guilt can cause you to cut off from your children and to have little contact, or if you do have contact, you can overcompensate with permissive parenting. These responses are not helpful to children and are motivated by strong negative emotions. It is important to start the healing process for yourself. The sooner you can accept what has happened, the sooner you can let go of bitterness, resentment and guilt, and the sooner you can be there for your children to help them cope.

HELPING CHILDREN COPE

For children, the conflict leading up to their parents' separation, the separation itself, and coming to terms with new living arrangements are all hugely stressful events. How they cope varies greatly according to their unique temperament, personality and individual needs. Each child is different. It is important that you listen carefully to them so that you can understand how they are coping, before you decide how best to help them. One very important factor determining children's coping is their age at the time their parents separate. Below are some guidelines as to how children of different ages experience their parents' separation and what you can do to help.

PRE-SCHOOLERS (0–4)
Pre-school children are generally upset and confused by their parents' separation. They find it hard to understand why it is happening and often experience it as a devastating blow to their sense of security. They often worry that if mum and dad have stopped loving each other, then they have stopped loving them too, or they fear that if one parent has left the home, then the other is likely to leave and abandon them also. They

often fantasise that they are in some way responsible for the separation, thinking, for example, that mum and dad have split up because they were bold. Pre-schoolers often demonstrate a lot of distressed behaviour, such as night fears, being over-clingy, tantrums, and disobedience. They do not have the words to describe how they feel and may instead 'act out' that distress in their behaviour.

How to help
Pre-school children need frequent reassurance that mum and dad both still love them, that they did nothing wrong to cause mum and dad to split up, and that they will be taken care of. These reassurances need to be frequent and in a simple language that children can easily understand. It is also very important that any changes of routine and living arrangements are explained clearly to pre-schoolers preferably in advance and by both parents. Just because pre-schoolers are younger, parents should not argue or criticise each other in front of them, assuming they don't understand what is being said. Even infants pick up on tensions and rows between parents and are adversely affected by them.

A good way to support pre-schoolers after separation is to make sure you spend one-to-one time with them, when you can listen to them, reassure them, and play with them. Don't 'compensate' with gifts or toys. What your children need most is your time, love and attention. In addition, young children need frequent contact with the parent who leaves. A gap of a week or two weeks is often far too long and can lead to huge anxiety. Pre-schoolers need frequent regular contact (especially in the immediate days after the separation) to reassure them that mum or dad still loves them and is there for them.

SCHOOL-AGE CHILDREN (5–10)

School-age children generally express a lot of grief, anger and sadness when their parents separate. They generally miss greatly the parent who has left the home (even if they had a poor relationship when he/she was there) and can express a lot of anger about this, sometimes taking it out on the parent who is left at home and caring for them. Though they are more able to understand the reasons for the separation, like younger children they can feel responsible and may fantasise and plan how they can get their parents back together again. They may think that if they behave very well, or indeed very badly, that they may somehow bring mum and dad back together.

Many of these children will hide their feelings (for example, saying they don't mind their parents separating, when in fact they feel terribly rejected and miss greatly the parent who has left) and appear to be coping initially, only to have lots of problems at later dates. Also, when there is serious conflict, some children will take sides, becoming an ally to the custodial parent against the parent who has left, and judging the separation in black and white terms. Often this is due to the children being sensitive to the custodial parents anger against the other parent, and their fear that they will be abandoned if they don't agree and tow the line.

YOU MUST BE PLEASED THAT YOUR MUM AND DAD CAN STILL AGREE ON SOME THINGS...

NOT WHEN THEY AGREE THAT I SHOULD WATCH LESS TELLY AND GET ON WITH MY HOMEWORK.

How to help
School-age children need honest and open communication from their parents about the separation. If there is no hope of a reconciliation this needs to be expressed clearly to them, while at the same time understanding their wish for a reunion. It is important that they are given space to express their feelings, especially their anger and upset. It is really helpful if as parents (custodial or non-custodial) you can listen to and take on board the upset and the complaints they have about you. Be really sensitive to children who appear to be unaffected by the separation. Make sure they still get special time and attention.

While you can acknowledge that mum and dad may disagree about some things, you should state clearly and repeatedly that you are both still parents to them and emphasise what you still agree about. It is important to work hard to get agreement with the other parent (see next chapter), and this, above all, helps the children to settle. At all costs, avoid putting children in the position where they have to 'take sides'. Give them permission to love the other parent, for example, by encouraging them to write, call or send cards. Be open to hearing your children talk positively about the other parent, without feeling resentment or jealousy. It really helps if you too can talk positively to them about the other parent.

As with younger children, it is very helpful to set aside special one-to-one time with your children on a regular or daily basis, when you can provide them with lots of positive attention by playing with them, listening to them, and being reassuring as appropriate.

YOUNG ADOLESCENTS (11+)

By adolescence, many youngsters are beginning to acquire the ability to think in a much more complicated way. They can now see not only what life is but also what it could or should be. They are also moving towards greater independence from the family and their peer group becomes very important as a reference point. While this increased independence and better intellectual and social resources can in some ways help adolescents cope with their parents' separation, it can also make things worse for them.

After separation, many adolescents can lose quality contact with one of their parents and this can lead to extra problems. Adolescence can be challenging at the best of times, but without the support of two involved parents these challenges can be greatly increased. Adolescents can feel very angry and upset at their parents' separation. They can cut off from their family, seeking the support of peers instead, and this can lead to anti-social behaviour if the peer group is unsuitable. In addition, teenagers can feel pressure to 'take sides' in parental conflict, and are even faced with choosing which parent they want to live with. Sometimes, distraught parents can over-depend on their adolescents emotionally. This can be a burden, making a teenager feel great guilt and worry. Being older, the needs of teenagers very often get missed out during separation.

How to help

Separated parents need to communicate honestly and openly with adolescents. Generally, teenagers value being told in an adult way, why and how the separation has happened. Remember that teenagers can appreciate that there are 'two sides to the story' and it can be very helpful to explain to them your views and feelings and then to objectively and fairly describe the other parent's views as well. This can relieve them of the burden of having to take sides and help them maintain a connection with both parents.

It is also crucial that parents work hard at connecting with and maintaining their relationship with their adolescents. Don't just assume they are okay; go out of your way to spend time with them and to talk and listen to them. It can be helpful if you can maintain a shared, enjoyable activity that you can do regularly with them (such as going to football, or shopping). Equally, parents need to supervise their teenagers in separated families every bit as much as in intact families. You do your teenagers no favours by being over-relaxed about rules or not taking normal precautions regarding safety (for example, knowing where they are).

Finally, avoid relying emotionally on your teenagers. As a separating parent you do need support and you need to seek this out (see Chapter 2). It is not, however, fair to expect youngsters to provide emotional supports to either parent or for them to take on the parenting role with younger children. Equally, make sure your teenagers have access to their own supports outside the family. Don't just leave it up to their peer group. If your teenager is upset, as well as providing support yourself, you could ask an extended family member or a trusted family friend who is popular with your teenager to adopt a supportive role.

HELPING CHILDREN COPE – SOME GENERAL PRINCIPLES

Breaking the news of the separation

Dealing with the actual separation and how to break the news to children can be one of the most difficult times for families. Below are some general guidelines. The emphasis and detail needs to be tailored to the particular child and his or her age and development. In general, it seems best to tell the children about the separation, but not until you are certain that the decision is final.

- Try to tell the children together and take time to plan what you are going to say.

- Choose a time when you can be with the children after breaking the news.

When Parents Separate

- Outline the main arrangements for their schooling, where and with whom they will live, where the other parent will live, and arrangements for ongoing contact with both parents and the extended family.

- Give a clear message that the separation is in no way the fault of the children and that there was nothing they could or should have done to stop it.

- Emphasise that although you, the parents, are separating, you will still be their parents. The conflict is between the parents, not between the parents and the children.

- Tell the children that both parents love them and that they will always be part of their lives.

- Check if the children have questions and be prepared to answer the same questions again over the next days, weeks and months.

- The children will need to manage the process of telling others, for example, friends at school. Parents should help them think through how they want to do this, and should give a clear message that it is not a secret or something of which the children should be ashamed.

Give the children the time and space to express their thoughts and feelings
Children will be upset, need reassurance and the opportunity to talk things through. It is normal and appropriate for children from separated families to feel sad and angry at times about the situation. While it may be hard to listen to, denying children

their negative feelings does not help. If you choose a time when you feel calm, then you will be able to let the children talk through their feelings without fearing that you will get angry, upset or critical. Children may need to repeat the same questions about the separation, although you feel you provided good answers the first time. Similarly, as they grow older and can understand more complex matters, they may want to ask different questions. It is best to see their questioning as a process. It may continue over a protracted period. An explanation at the time of the separation is unlikely to be sufficient in the longer term. It is as well to remember that if you feel unable to respond to questioning, then maybe there is another adult around who can do so until you feel ready. Ideally, both parents should be emotionally and physically available to talk openly and honestly to the children.

Minimise the life changes your child has to endure
When parents separate, much of the trauma children suffer is not directly due to the separation itself, but rather on account of the life changes that often occur. Children may experience disruptive changes such as living in a different house, moving far away to a new area, changing schools, or losing contact with friends and extended family members, etc. It is important that these changes be minimised. You may think that moving to a new city will be a fresh start for you and your new family, but you may serve your children better by keeping things stable in their lives, at least for the first few years after the separation. If some changes are inevitable (and they often are) try and maintain other sources of stability in your children's lives. For example, you may have to move house, but your children could stay in the same school, though they may have to travel a little further to get there.

Maintain the quality of your parenting
In the difficult times of separation, and without the support of a partner, it is easy for parents to let the quality of their parenting slip. Your children, however, need consistent and loving parenting more than ever during this time. They need your encouragement, love and attention as well as your rules, guidance and boundaries, as much if not more than before. Below are some ideas on positive parenting that you can apply in your family.

1. Try and spend individual time with each of your children, when you can play with them, relax and enjoy each other's company.

2. Spend family time together weekly, using the time to plan, discuss rules and chores and to have fun.

3. Set clear rules with your children and enforce them calmly by using consequences to help them learn to take responsibility (e.g. if your child does not come in on time, then he doesn't go out the next day).

4. Be consistent in your routines and reliable in any promises or arrangements you make. This is especially critical for children who need to rebuild their sense of security.

For more ideas on positive parenting, please see the books *Bringing up Responsible Children* and *Bringing up Responsible Teenagers* that are listed at the end of this book.

Accept the other parent's role in your child's life
Though your former partner may not be an important person in

your own life, he/she is likely to be a very important person in your child's life. Being a good parent means accepting the other parent's role in your child's life and taking steps to support their involvement. See their involvement as an advantage. It is good for children to have two different adults (though living apart) caring for them and involved in their lives. It can also be an advantage for you in helping you share the many responsibilities of bringing up a child. See your child's time with the other parent not as an intrusion, but as a benefit to your child and a 'break' for you.

Don't bad-mouth or criticise the other parent in front of the children
While you may feel very negatively about your former partner, it is very distressing for the children to hear frequent criticism of someone that they almost certainly still love and probably greatly miss. Save expressions of frustration and negative feelings for when you talk to other adults who are supporting you and try to speak positively (or at least neutrally) about the other parent in front of your children. It is crucial that you don't compete with your former partner for your children's love, and that you don't put your children in a position where they feel they have to take sides. Forcing your children to take sides is damaging to them. Above all, your children need to know that it is all right for them to love both of you.

Don't use your children as 'go-betweens'
Children in separated families, especially when parents are still very angry with each other, should not be used as 'go-betweens' between adults or as 'spies' on the former partner. While you may feel your former partner is behaving in a totally unreasonable manner, it is not in any way your children's responsibility to serve as a line of communication between you and him or her. Children placed in this position find it very difficult and report that it is very distressing for them. You are the parents, it is up to you to find a way of dealing with practical adult decisions (see the next chapter on negotiating conflict). Similarly, it is very unhelpful to ask your children to 'spy' on your former partner. If the relationship between the adults is over then each should be free to get on with a new life.

A FINAL POINT
In this chapter we have concentrated on helping children cope with the negative effects of their parents separation. Research suggests, however, that it is *excessive conflict between parents, whether they are living together or not, which seems to have the most damaging effect on children.* Indeed, some children may actually blossom post-separation if this means they are relieved from the stresses of living with two parents in conflict, and they can go on to live in a less neglectful, less abusive and more harmonious family environment. Of course, this is not to underestimate the often very considerable stress caused by separation and divorce that many children and their families feel.

In the next chapter we look at what you can do to reduce and manage the conflict between you and the other parent, so as to best serve the interests of your children.

CO-PARENTING/NEGOTIATING
WITH THE OTHER PARENT

If you didn't have children together, separating from your partner would be easier. You could move away, put your past relationship behind you and get on with the rest of your life with little or no contact with your ex. Having children, however, changes everything. Generally, children need the support and involvement of both their parents, which means that not only will you have on-going contact with your former partner, but also that you have a responsibility to develop a working co-parenting relationship with them. Though this can be very difficult, this is perhaps the single most important thing you can do for your children to help them cope with the separation of their parents. Excessive conflict and ongoing disputes between parents after separation is devastating to children. They easily get caught up in the middle and their relationship with both parents is damaged. Be wary of trying to win one over on your former partner or aiming to gain victory by going to court. The adversarial nature of the court system can increase conflict and bitterness, which can endure far beyond the time a judge has imposed a settlement. The best thing you can do for your children is to learn to negotiate with the other parent and to reach agreement/compromise on important matters concerning your children such as access, money, schooling, etc. One way to this is by learning to develop a business relationship with your former partner

Developing a 'Business-Like' Relationship
Isolina Ricci (1997) writes about how most of the conflict between parents post-separation is caused by one or both of

them still expecting to relate to the other on an intimate level, as if they were still married or in a close intimate relationship. This can lead to great hurt being expressed and unhelpful expectations being created. She argues that the best solution is for parents to withdraw from having an intimate relationship and to create a new working relationship that is more business-like. It is better to relate to your former partner as if they were an important colleague in a work context. You may not be best friends and you may not be emotionally close, but you are bound together in an extremely important shared business goal – parenting your children. The personal relationship has ended, but the business of parenting continues, and it is crucial that you find a new business-like way of relating. The more you are able to do that, the better for your children. The following are the principles of building an effective business-like relationship with your former partner

*Maintain your independence and respect
the other parent's independence also*
Although you are co-parents, you also have separate lives and separate homes. Just as in a work setting where business and private lives are kept separate, so it can be in your relationship with your former partner. If achieved, this can be a relief,

especially if you have been in constant conflict. Remember, your involvement with your former partner is time-limited and focused on parenting and the needs of your children. In addition, accept the fact that you and the other parent will have different styles of parenting. There will be different rules in each of your houses, different routines and a different way of relating to your children. While you will have to agree on some important matters, it is okay for things to be different and children can cope with this quite well. It is more important to children to see their parents relating respectfully to one another than for every rule to be consistent and agreed.

Keep your feelings in check
Don't ask too much about your former partner's personal life and feelings, and don't over disclose about your own personal matters either. This means that if you feel upset at being alone or feel jealous of your former partner's new relationship, do not talk to him/her about these feelings, rather set some time aside to share these with a close friend. In addition, don't let your anger or frustration get the better of you. If you do so, you are likely to evoke an angry or defensive response and stop any positive negotiation. Effective negotiators never lose control of their feelings. They remain calm and put their anger and frustration to one side.

Keep your communication focused
on the present and the needs of your children
When conflict is high it is hard to stay focused on the needs of your children. Parents can get distracted easily by past hurts and other grievances and bring up non-parenting issues instead. It is important that you resist this temptation and that you focus

clearly on the present and what you want for your children. Equally, don't take the bait if your former partner 'presses your button' and brings up an old argument. Instead, politely re-focus the discussion, for example, by saying 'I'm not going to talk about that now, I simply rang to fix a time for me to collect Sue.'

Do communicate directly and openly with the other parent
If you have something to say to the other parent that is relevant to the business of co-parenting, then it is important that you communicate this to them directly, either face to face, by telephone, or even by note. Be wary of communicating indirectly by asking someone else to tell them, and it is certainly unfair to use your children as 'go-betweens'. If you need to

change a time of a visit, then ring the other parent to discuss this. If this is difficult you could consider writing a note, but don't ask your children to negotiate on your behalf.

Negotiating with the Other Parent

Learning to negotiate with the other parent over important parenting issues, and coming to acceptable agreements about your children's care, is a crucial step in helping them cope with the separation. As stated before, this is often very difficult to achieve, and we suggest a number of 'negotiation principles' that can help this come about.

1) Pick a good time to negotiate

Negotiation works best when you are both calm and have enough time to talk. If you have an issue that you need to negotiate with the other parent about, think carefully about when and where to do this. It is probably not a good time to raise it when you are angry or upset. For example, if the other parent is consistently late picking up the children for access, leaving you dealing with anxious and waiting children, confronting him/her on the doorstep in front of the children, when you are both pressured and your blood is beginning to boil, is probably not a good idea. It might be better to plan to ring later about it or to ask 'I need to talk to you about the collecting arrangements, when would be a good time to ring?'

LET'S NEGOTIATE ABOUT WHO HAS THE KIDS AT THE WEEKEND... BUT NOT THIS WEEKEND BECAUSE I'VE GOT THE KIDS OVER.

2) Listen first

Effective negotiators always take steps to understand and appreciate the other person's point of view before they communicate their own thoughts. This can be hard if you're in conflict all the time. The most important skill in reducing conflict is listening. If you can listen and show you appreciate the other parent's point of view, then they are more likely to listen and take on board your views also. Listening is not about agreeing or giving up your own position, it is simply about understanding. For example, even though you feel financially stretched paying child support and living in a small apartment, you can still appreciate the financial burden of your former partner living as a single parent. Or even though you deal with the kids all day long and feel burdened by this, you can still appreciate the distance your former partner has to travel in traffic to get there on time.

3) Give your view respectfully
When giving your point of view, make sure you do it in a way that is respectful and assertive. Avoid harassing, threatening or insulting the other parent and try not to blame or over-criticise. None of these tactics will help matters, but they can be very damaging. Be positive and calm when you express your point of view, take responsibility for your feelings and express what you want to happen. Consider the following examples:

Ineffective: You're deliberately changing the access times to try and stop me seeing the kids. You've no right. *(attacking and blaming 'you' message)*

Effective: The change of time doesn't suit me because of my work. I would prefer if we kept them at the same time. *(gives clear explanation and states what he/she wants)*

Ineffective: You're so inconsiderate. You never think to get the children to do their homework on the weekend. It's just all fun for you, and I'm left to force them to do it when they're tired. *(sarcastic, blaming)*

Effective: Listen, I appreciate that you like to do fun things over the weekend with the kids, but it is important that they do their homework as well. Can you arrange a time to do it with them over the weekend? *(states positive first and then makes a clear reasonable request)*

4) Think of mutually beneficial solutions

The final stage of negotiation is to try to come up with solutions and agreements that are beneficial to both you and the other parent. This is very different from gaining a 'victory' over your former partner or proving that they were wrong. Both of these strategies are short-sighted, making it unlikely that your former partner will co-operate in the future. It is rather about finding a way of accommodating both your points of view through a solution that you both accept. In the homework example above, for instance, the parents may come up with the following solution: the first parent does some of the homework with the children before they go away on the weekend, the second parent makes sure to complete it with the kids on Sunday before they return to the first parent, who arranges a quiet evening in with them. With this solution, parents share in both the fun and the responsible times (homework) in caring for the children. Finding mutually beneficial solutions is often simply about negotiating satisfactory compromises. For example, a father may agree to let the children have 'his' Saturday with the mother, because she has a special family event. But the mother agrees to return the favour the following month when the father wants to take the kids away for an extended weekend.

WE CAN'T AGREE ON WHICH MEDIATION SERVICE TO USE...

Professional mediation service

How to Negotiate when the Other Parent is Unreasonable
In the hurt and bitterness of separation, it is very common for parents to behave unreasonably at times, either by refusing to negotiate or by becoming excessively hostile. During those times it can be important to take a break from negotiations and to try again at another time. In time, strong emotions can settle down and people can become more open to discussion.

If you have difficulty talking directly to each other, you can seek the help of a professional mediation service (see Useful Contacts at the back of the booklet). A mediator will meet with both of you and try to help you come up with a working parenting agreement. In addition, you can also seek legal help via a solicitor and go to court to resolve your dispute. A judge can establish a schedule of contact or strongly encourage you to go to mediation, or request an outside expert to assess what is best for your children. Sometimes, in circumstances of high-conflict, a court order can be helpful in fixing the times of contact and the amount of access where parents are unable to negotiate this directly. One should be cautious about using the court system excessively, however, as its adversarial nature of court can aggravate rather than reduce conflict.

In a minority of cases (for example, when there has been abuse or physical violence) it may not be possible or advisable for you to negotiate with your former partner. In those cases, you could seek the support of professional services such as those listed in the back of the booklet.

BEING A SINGLE PARENT

THE CHALLENGES

Post separation, many parents (usually mothers) suddenly find themselves in the role of being a single parent; they are now almost single-handedly responsible for the daily care of their children, with all the struggles and stresses this brings. While children are not necessarily worse off because they live in a single parent family (and indeed there can be advantages if the new arrangement relieves children of being in an excessively conflictual home situation), single parenthood brings considerable challenges and stresses:

- Reduced income, due to the increased childcare costs and the need to maintain two homes.

- Loss of an ally and co-parent. The multiple demands of busy family life still have to be managed, but now with one less 'pair of hands'.

- Less personal and social time for you. There will be fewer breaks and opportunities for you to relax and look after your own needs, even though the parenting demands on you have increased.

- Managing the children's distress alone. Children who are upset and angry at their parents' separation often only express their feelings to the parent caring for them on a daily basis. You are likely to get the brunt of their distress and have to deal with many discipline issues alone.

RISING TO THE CHALLENGE

Work constructively with the other parent
As discussed in the last chapter, there are clear advantages to maintaining a civil and business-like relationship with your former partner. Children do best when the 'live-away' parent remains supportively involved and in contact with them. For example, research has shown that children from single parent families (headed by the mother) do better academically when fathers are actively involved in their children's schooling, for example, by attending teacher-parent meetings. In simple terms, children do better when they have two concerned and interested parents involved in their lives

In addition, the involvement of the other parent can have advantages for you in reducing the burden of being a single parent. If your former partner takes a more extensive childcare role, then you will have more time to yourself to recharge and to pursue your own social interests. Secondly, you will have reduced childcare costs because you don't have to pay a baby-sitter and because 'live-away' parents who remain emotionally involved in their children's lives are much more likely to pay child support and to support their children financially as they become adults (e.g. when they go to college). Finally, children who are in contact with the other parent (and this is particularly the case for boys and their fathers) can be helped settle more quickly after the separation and may be less likely to have discipline problems.

For all these reasons it is worth working hard to facilitate the involvement of the other parent in your children's lives even though you have separated. While this is not always within your control (many live-away parents drift apart from their children despite the best intentions of the custodial parent), certainly don't put up any unnecessary obstacles to the other parent remaining involved. For example, you may be tempted to punish your former partner by restricting access, but this does not serve your children's or your own interests in the long term. Even if your former partner, in your view, took on few childcare responsibilities when s/he was living at home, this does not mean that they could not take on parenting responsibilities when separated. Most 'live-away' parents can quickly learn these tasks in the period following separation.

It is also your right to insist that your former partner takes on their fair share of the childcare responsibilities. It is generally the best for your child, and relieves you of some of the burdens of being a single parent. For ideas on how to negotiate with your former partner about co-parenting, see chapter 4.

Be organised

Parents generally need to be organised, but single parents who head up households really need to be organised. It has already been suggested that separated parents should try and develop a business-like relationship with each other, but it can also help to think of the family as a business. Businesses need to plan ahead and so do single parents!

Each evening draw up a plan for the next day. Note down which jobs are essential, which are desirable, and which can really wait. Daily planning will help you avoid things like the morning scramble. It may also help with your own sleep because you don't need to lay awake trying to remember all the tasks you have to do the next day!

Once a week sit down with the children and plan for the medium term. Medium term planning means you don't lose sight of the bigger picture and the less frequent but important family events like holiday and birthday planning. Successful businesses have good filing systems. They know where to find important information. In families, a lot of time can be lost and plenty of hassle experienced in looking for bills, forms and receipts – so make sure to keep track of everything.

Maintain the quality of your parenting
Under the stress of single parenthood, it is easy to let the quality of your parenting slip. You may suddenly find yourself having to be both 'mother and father' to the children, being nurturing and

kind as well as firm and authoritarian. This can be difficult if you deferred some of these roles to your former partner, for example, if s/he was the main nurturer, or the parent who looked after discipline. In addition, children can present a lot of discipline problems after their parents' separation and need firm and loving parenting more than ever. So it is really important that you get the support you need to maintain the quality of your parenting. This includes setting individual time aside to listen, talk and play with your children, being consistent in your rules and routines, and being calm and firm when you enforce rules. See chapter 3, or some of the further reading listed at the end for more ideas.

Seek the support you need
It is hard being a parent alone, so it is really important that you seek the support you need. Extended family members, friends, and neighbours can be all great sources of practical and emotional support as you take on the task of single parenthood. You might also find a lot of resources (such as parents' groups or family resource centres) in your local community that may be helpful to you. For example, some parents cope by sharing tasks such as the school run with other parents. A good idea is to sit down and to make a list of the supports you need, what is available and who can help.

As stated before, don't forget to work constructively with the children's other parent to ensure they take on some of the childcare responsibilities. This is often the best arrangement for your children, who gain contact with their 'live-away' parent while you can pursue other things.

Finally, it is also reasonable to expect children, especially the older ones, to play a role in looking after household responsibilities. You may even find that this sharing of responsibility gives the children a sense of importance and enhanced worth. Sharing the responsibility may also help to bond the new and smaller unit and may give everybody a better sense of stability, which is probably much needed following the transition to being a single parent family.

TRICKY SITUATIONS AND WHAT TO DO ABOUT THEM

When you row every time you meet the other parent
Sometimes separation and divorce can be very messy. The feelings of hurt and anger can last well beyond the actual split and spill out each time you meet. If the other parent is to continue to play a role in the child's life, and usually this is a good idea, then you really need to work on creating a civil, business-like relationship with them. Here are some useful ideas for you to try. Firstly, organise that the hand-over of children occurs in a public place. This reduces the chances of there being an open row. Secondly, you may find it better to deliver rather than collect the children. Delivering leaves less time for hanging around, and thus less space for that row to develop. Thirdly, communicate important information — changes in the child's medication, the time of hockey practice — in writing, but keep it factual. We have already emphasised how important it is to avoid using the children as the message carrier and for them to be kept clear of parental rows. Finally, if difficulties persist, it is worth seeking professional help in the form of a family counsellor or a mediator who can help you and your former partner to come to a workable agreement (see also chapter 4 for more ideas).

When the other parent is unreliable
Children in separated families can be hurt and can get very angry when their parents fail to keep to arrangements. When their live-away parent doesn't turn up on a regular basis children often conclude that they are not loved by him/her.

If access arrangements are not working out then the first step is for the parents to try and discuss the issues and to negotiate a different arrangement that suits everyone. If it is not possible to negotiate a more reliable arrangement with the other parent you should negotiate a 'Plan B' with the children. Plan B might specify how long they would wait for the live-away parent to arrive and what alternative activities are available should the promised arrival not occur. This sort of 'Plan B' approach can often provide much relief for children and help them cope with the uncertain access arrangements.

In many cases it is not possible to negotiate satisfactory visiting arrangements with the live-away parent. As stated earlier, many live-away parents can drift out of their children's lives despite the best intentions of the custodial parent to maintain their involvement. In these situations it is important to

When Parents Separate

be sensitive to your children's feelings. They may feel upset, disappointed and angry at the other parent's lack of involvement and will need you to listen and support them. Be careful not to express your own angry feelings about the other parent by bad-mouthing them, but rather try and listen and give a balanced account of the reasons for their other parent's lack of involvement. In addition, be open to the fact that the level of contact between your children and the other parent may change over time. For example, it is common as their own circumstances change, for live-away parents to try to restart or increase contact with their children. It is important that you are open to this idea and available to negotiate it carefully in the best interests of your children.

Equally, your children may wish to initiate contact with the live-away parent themselves, for example, by writing a letter or making a telephone call. Indeed, it is very common for children as they become older to become interested in the parent they have lost touch with and to want to make new efforts to contact him/her. As the custodial parent, your children will need your support and guidance if contact with the live-away parent is to restart in a helpful way.

Should I get a job outside the home?
There are pros and cons. Work outside the home can certainly provide benefits: you get to socialise with other adults; you acquire a new role in life; and work brings cash and easier access to credit facilities. But there are disadvantages too. Just arranging good childcare can be a difficult issue for many working parents, never mind being able to afford it. There can be other work-related expenses too, for example, the cost of transport to and from work, the cost of clothes for work and eating your lunch

out. And if you work outside the home the housework doesn't go away. You have to squeeze it in at another time. You also have to plan for what happens if your child is sick. It would be wise to check carefully whether the overall benefits to you of working are not outweighed by the loss of financial benefits from the state. Some parents find a happy medium in finding part-time work or a job with flexible hours which they can balance around their busy life as a single parent.

Are there times when I should seek help from professionals?
The simple answer is yes. If you've tried negotiating with the other parent on important issues and had insufficient success then maybe you should think about going to a professional counsellor or mediator or consulting a solicitor. If you feel you are not managing, and are getting overwhelmed, then talk to a reliable friend or a sensible relative, or seek some professional support, perhaps from your GP. If the children are really not settling, then maybe they need to see a counsellor with you or on their own.

BEING A 'LIVE-AWAY' PARENT

Post separation, the most common living arrangement is for the children to live with one parent (usually the mother) and for the other parent (usually the father) to live away, but to have contact with the children. This level of contact can vary greatly. In the chaotic time just after separation contact can be sporadic or even cease for a period (sadly, just when children, especially younger ones, need most reassurance from the parent who has left). Over time the situation can stabilise and many live-away parents are successful in achieving good quality, regular contact with their children. It is often difficult for this contact to be maintained, however, and there is a

tendency for it to wane and to eventually stop. In research studies, nearly half of the parents who live away from their children post separation lose contact altogether with their children within a few years.

While these parents are often characterised as selfish or not caring of their children, this does not take into account the obstacles and difficulties live-away parents face when they attempt to maintain supportive contact. Many struggle with their own personal pain and the practical difficulties such as finding accommodation and tight finances. They often find themselves at great disadvantage in the courts, with their former partner who lives with the children 'holding all the cards'. Others feel great guilt or hurt at the separation and this prevents them from having contact with the children as this will bring them into contact with their former partner. Others wonder if they have anything of value to offer their children and often think their children would be better off without them.

Despite these obstacles, however, many live-away parents are successful in creating a stable situation where they work with their former partner to have regular quality contact with their children, and are a positive influence as their children grow up. In the next section we outline some important principles in achieving this.

STAYING SUPPORTIVELY INVOLVED

Staying connected with your children and supportively involved in their lives is difficult at the best of times, even when you live with the other parent. It becomes especially difficult if you are a live-away parent and you have to work harder to maintain a positive connection.

Co-operate with your former partner

We have already emphasised how important it is for you to develop a co-operative, 'business-like' relationship with your former partner for the sake of your children. This is especially the case if you are the live-away parent. It will be very difficult for you to maintain a quality relationship with your children unless, on some level, you have the support of your former partner, who is living with your children daily and has a strong influence on them. Perhaps the single biggest reason live-away parents stop having contact with their children is due to on-going conflict with the children's live-in parent. It is important to take steps to reduce this conflict and to negotiate with your former partner. As described in the last chapter, this is not about giving in to your former partner on every issue or accepting unreasonable demands, but it is about understanding their perspective, persisting in communicating your point of view and seeking compromise and mutually beneficial solutions.

Live-away parents often feel they are in a weaker position than that of the other parent, who can call all the shots. In such instances, there is the option of seeking support from the court system. Except in exceptional cases, a judge will grant 'reasonable' access to a live-away parent and in many instances they are prepared to consider shared custody, giving parents equal responsibility. Though we are wary of the adversarial nature of courts, in many high conflict situations a court order regularising contact arrangements can help settle and stabilise matters. Even when a court order has been granted, it is still important to work on building a co-operative civil relationship with your former partner. If you find yourself constantly fighting with your former partner, you are indirectly fighting your kids, who more often than not are caught in the middle of this conflict.

Keep your promises
Keeping promises with children is important. It becomes especially so when you live away from them following a separation. When you lived with your children you might have been flexible or loose about when you would take them out or read them a bedtime story. After separation it is important to be

much more definite and consistent. Children can be devastated if their parent is late or, worse still, does not turn up for an agreed activity, or forgets to make the promised telephone call. The regularity of these actions help children feel secure and loved and ensure you remain connected and involved. This is why it is important to only make promises that you can keep. Don't arrange to call at a time when you are likely to be busy, or pick a visit time that is impossible due to a lengthy travel time.

If you cannot keep contact time or are going to be late, tell your child in advance and make alternative arrangements. It's also important to say sorry if you have let your child down. This can be very helpful to children in showing how seriously you rate spending time with them.

It can be helpful to plan your time together in advance, for when you do meet. You could chat with your child about what you are going to do, and even draw up a master list of activities you both enjoy or places you both like to visit. Focus on having a pleasant relaxed time together rather than a frantic rush to fit everything in, and remember, it doesn't have to be expensive to be fun – most children value their parents' time and attention more than anything else.

Be a responsible parent

When you do see your children it is natural to want to try and make it a fun and enjoyable experience, full of nice trips and activities. However, it is also important not to shirk on parenting responsibilities such as helping children with homework, setting rules and ensuring they go to bed on time. Your children will respect you greatly as they grow up if you take your fair share of the responsible side of parenting (as well as the fun side). Equally, this is the best way to co-operate with their live-in parent. For example, it is very common for children to have some behavioural problems post-separation and to take a lot of their anger out on the parent they live with. If your former partner is struggling with a discipline issue, don't use this as an opportunity to blame her or to point out how you would be better at handling the problem, but support her instead. Work together to solve the problem through adopting a common discipline approach. If as a father you discover that your son is rude and aggressive to his mother, you could, on discussion with her, sit down with him and explain that you don't tolerate such behaviour, that you want him to find other ways to express his anger and that he must be more respectful to his mother. Similarly, if your daughter is falling behind on her grades, make sure to schedule time to do homework with her when she visits.

Be creative about how you stay in touch

Face to face contact isn't the only way to keep in touch with your children. There are many other creative ways listed below that can be invaluable, especially if you live far away from your children and regular face to face contact is not possible.

- *Email*

  It's quite easy to keep in contact with people nowadays, even over long distances. The advent of email means you can be in daily contact, keeping up to date with what is happening in your children's lives, answering questions and reassuring them about what's happening in your life, all at minimal expense.

- *Phoning*

  The phone is better still and it's worth phoning children regularly at an agreed time each week. Some children, particularly younger ones, find it hard to talk over the phone and wonder what they should chat to you about. It's worth noting down topics before you lift the receiver, for example, who they are meeting/playing with, how school is going, or what they've been doing in their spare time. With older children you and they can keep a diary through the week, noting down things you want to tell each other. You know when you'll be phoning so make sure you are in 'good form' and keep the atmosphere upbeat. Be open to what your children may be bothered about and want to discuss with you, but don't load them with your worries, concerns, regrets or loneliness. Focus on their needs, not your feelings. Your children are not there as your support.

- *Snail mail*

  In the electronic era it's perhaps even more pleasant to receive something through the post. It's worth buying a selection of cards in one go and then you can send them at intervals. Sending small gifts in the post when they're not expected, just to reassure the child that s/he is in your thoughts, is a very good investment. If you provide a pack of stamped addressed envelopes for the child to send notes to you this may also help them to feel more in touch.

- *Other ways to stay connected*
    1. For younger children you can tape record yourself reading bedtime stories.
    2. With older children you can write or invent stories for them to read, which you can send them in the post.
    3. Chat about books you and the child are reading at the same time, or about a TV programme or a match you've both watched.
    4. Go out and buy copies of your child's school books or the games they like so you know what they are doing and thinking about.
    5. Send daily postcards when you go on holidays.
    6. Keep a diary of what is happening in your life and save it for your children for when they are older.
    7. Use photos. Tell the child where you have put theirs and maybe take photos when you have outings together for them to keep as a reminder.

Whether you live far away from your children or not, creative ways of staying in contact can be touching to them and extremely valuable in getting the message across that you are there for them, that you are thinking of them and that you love them.

Don't be disheartened by rejection
Live-away parents often become disheartened when their children seem at times uninterested in their visits or contact. You might go to great effort to ring at a certain time only to be told by your daughter that she wants to return to watching her favourite TV programme. Or you might be upset that your children never write back to your weekly letters and cards and be tempted to stop writing. It is important to remember, however, that this is quite normal. Even in 'live-together' families, children can take their parents' attention for granted. It is quite normal for older children and teenagers to want to spend more time with their friends and to become more interested in activities outside the family.

What is important is that you don't take this apparent 'lack of interest' personally or interpret it as a sign to stop making efforts to keep in contact. Rather it is important to be flexible about contact, making an effort to fit it in with all the other activities and interests in your children's lives. In addition, it is unreasonable to expect young children (and even teenagers) to make efforts to contact you or to always respond to your initiatives. It is your responsibility to keep contact going and this will stand to you in the long term as your children become adults and they realise the efforts you made to be there for them and to stay involved in their lives.

Be patient if restarting contact

For different reasons, many live-away parents lose contact with their children. They can find themselves in the position of wondering whether to restart contact and how to go about this. This is a very delicate issue. Children can be very angry at a parent who they perceive at having abandoned them and, depending on their age, they may also have moved on to create a new life for themselves. In restarting contact it is important to go slow and to be patient. Think through what role you are prepared to have in your child's life and don't restart contact if you are not able to maintain it or to become supportively involved.

Before restarting contact, you will first have to discuss with your child's live-in parent about how to do it, and this can take some time and delicate negotiation (either directly, via mediation, or via court). Once this is done, it may be a good idea to restart contact with your children in stages, by writing to them for a period before meeting them. Whatever way you start contact, be prepared for the fact that you may have to apologise for not keeping contact in the past, and remember that it will take time to rebuild their trust and a new relationship with them.

NEW RELATIONSHIPS AND STEP-FAMILIES

After separation, many parents go on to form relationships with new partners. It is perfectly reasonable that parents should have a social life and that they move on in this way. However, introducing new significant people into children's lives is a tricky process and can be fraught with difficulties. Below are a number of guidelines to help you take your children's needs into account as you embark on dating, making new relationships and forming step-families.

STARTING TO DATE AND MAKE NEW RELATIONSHIPS

Reassure the children repeatedly, by word and deed, that dating doesn't affect your love for them or mean they are taking second place. Children who have experienced separation and divorce are naturally concerned about being abandoned and about losing you. If you are dating, then there is even more need for you to set aside special time to remain well connected with your children. Don't jump feet first into a new relationship. Take it slowly. It has to be a package deal. If the new partner isn't keen on children or the idea of an instant family then it's best to call a halt early on.

OF COURSE I DON'T MIND IF YOU START DATING, DAD - YOU LOOK PRETTY DATED TO ME ANYWAY!

Children shouldn't be present when you are dating a new person. Quite apart from the fact that it is about adults relating, the relationship may not last, and exposing children to a string of different partners leads them to feel confused and uncertain. It's best early on that your dating takes place outside the home, and only in the home when the children are away (for example, staying with the other parent). Give your children plenty of time to get used to the idea that you have a new partner before the first face to face meeting takes place.

When your children have met your new partner, be open to their opinions and listen to what they have to say about the new person. It is understandable that they may have very mixed feelings about there being another adult in your life. You may even be introducing this new person before the children have completely sorted out issues to do with their other parent and your separation. Accept that teenagers may not want to spend much time with parents, let alone with their parent's new partner.

STEP-FAMILIES

Adults and children who join together as a step-family face significant challenges. Learning to live and get on with a new set of people can be fraught with 'teething problems'. Children can feel jealous at having to share their parents, or left out and insecure in the new living arrangements. Becoming a happy and harmonious step-family isn't easy and special planning and preparation is required. A useful first question for the adults to ask is what does it look like from where the children are standing?

Children joining a new step-family bring with them the experience of family breakdown and possibly of marital conflict, and certainly a sense of loss. The new union may mean that they have to move away from their familiar friends, from their old school, neighbourhood and extended family.

Children joining a new family may also be required to share their space with the step-parent's own children. At the very least they will now very clearly be sharing their parent with another adult. For older children this may also mean giving up some of the more grown-up responsibility they took on, or were given, when their biological parents' relationship broke down. For all children, a new union is further proof that their biological parents will not be getting back together gain. That realisation may provoke another bout of grieving.

As if these changes weren't enough, children may feel that they share some of the responsibility for the breakdown of the relationship between their biological parents. They may fear being rejected or disliked by the new step-parent, and worry about the implications of that for their relationship with the custodial parent. Children are likely to have had little or no say in whether this new family should form. They know that things can go badly wrong in families and here they are entering another.

When Parents Separate

What can the Adults do to Help?

The custodial parent
- *Take it slow and be understanding*
  Your children may be initially reluctant and unsure about the new family arrangements and will need a lot of time to come to terms with it. Listen to their feelings and wishes and, as far as possible, take these into account when you plan for the future.

- *Support your children's relationship with the other parent*
  Don't see the family arrangements as an opportunity to 'cut loose' or reduce contact with the other parent. Children often need a lot of reassurance during this time that their other parent will continue to be involved in their lives. It's a big help if you can maintain a good co-parenting relationship and communicate and negotiate directly with the other parent to facilitate the children keeping in touch.

- *Make sure you spend individual time with your children*
  Many children spend less individual time with their birth parent in a new family and miss this greatly. Don't insist that your new partner or new step-children become involved in all family activities you spend with your children. Set aside special time and activities when you can be alone with your children to listen and talk to them and to simply enjoy each others company. In preparing to form a step-family, it can be helpful to have a series of family talks with the 'original family' (i.e. you and your children) before introducing your new partner and step-children to the discussions.

- *Work on developing a good relationship with your new partner*
  It is helpful if your children see that you have a supportive relationship with your new partner and that it leads to more harmony for all. If you are going to have an argument with your new partner then try to hold it until the children are not around. Arguments may be particularly worrying for them if they were associated with the breakdown of your relationship with their other parent.

  Open communication between the new couple about their own parenting style, standards and expectations, and particularly good communication and problem-solving about how their differing styles can be merged, is essential to success. Mutual support for each other creates a climate of security for the children. How the new couple negotiate and resolve their differences can also serve as a very useful learning experience for children, and a model for how the children can usefully play their part in forming the new family.

The live-away parent

- *Accept the role of the new step-parent in your children's lives*
  It is very helpful if you can accept that there is now a new adult in your child's life and that you do not 'compete' or be negative about them. Your child should feel free to mention their new step-parent without having to fear your reaction. Even more than this, your child may need your support to form a relationship with the step-parent and know that s/he is not being disloyal to you by doing so.

  Remember the arrival of a step-parent can have a number of advantages for your child. By providing support to the other parent the step-parent can often help create more security and stability for your child, and indeed may form a supportive friendship with your child that is another resource for him/her.

- *Maintain your own supportive involvement*
  Though the arrival of a new step-parent does bring changes, it need not drastically alter your relationship with your children. Though you may need to negotiate with the other parent about the new living arrangements and be flexible about how you maintain contact, you should work hard to ensure you remain involved. Rather than 'backing off' to give the family space, children often need you more during these times, and they can become very distressed when parents do not visit or phone at the agreed time. Show by your actions as well as your words that your feelings for your children have not and will not change.

The new step-parent
- *Take time to build a relationship with your partner's children*
  As a step-parent you will have a very different relationship with your partner's children to what they have with their birth parents. While young children may begin to relate to you in a parenting role, older children are likely to have much more mixed feelings. Many children will see you not as their step-parent but as their mother's or father's new partner. Give the children space to work out their feelings and don't put them under any pressure. Respect their relationship with their live-away parent and avoid competing or trying to replace this parent's involvement.

  Young children are capable of developing good strong attachments with both types of parents. However, a good relationship between a child and a new step-parent will take time to develop. It would be nice if happy families could be created instantly, but that's not what happens in the real world. Some experts suggest that the process can take between two and five years.

- *Initially become a 'supportive friend' to your new step-children*
A good way to start is to try and build a 'supportive friendship' with your step-child. Don't immediately leap into the role of being a parent, but spend some time getting to know them and understanding what their concerns and interests are. It can be a good idea to try and develop a shared interest with them, but let this evolve naturally. It can be much harder with older children and teenagers who are unsure about what type of relationship they want to have with you. Expect initial rejection and don't take it personally. Be patient and persistent in trying to become friends with them.

- *Don't get too involved initially in discipline*
Children, especially the older ones, are likely to resent it if you immediately take on a discipline role with them. It is best initially to leave this to their birth parents and for you to adopt a supportive role to your partner and the children as they work out discipline issues. As you develop a more trusting relationship with the children, you will be able to assume a more central parenting role, especially if the children are younger. With older children and teenagers, however, who are already moving towards independence, this may not happen, and it is best to simply maintain a supportive role.

- *Work on developing a good relationship with your new partner*
  A new step-parent may feel like an outsider at first, realising that they are not part of much of the history and shared experience between their new partner and his/her children. Time and experience will create a new, shared family history. In the meantime, it is particularly important for the new couple to work hard on strengthening their own bond so that there is a secure base from which they and the children can build this shared positive experience.

MOVING THINGS FORWARD

People enter step-families with a history of traditions, experiences and expectations. These may not be immediately apparent. From time to time the new family members may be quite surprised to find that much of what they take for granted is not universally accepted as the way to do things. It is likely that new rituals, rules and ways of behaving will have to be developed.

Getting to know each other

It is really important to set aside time for the new family members to talk, share and to get to know one another. This can be done by having a sit down mealtime without the TV, or by being around to chat when the children come in from school. Regular family meetings can also be very helpful. These meetings can be used to discuss routines and family rules, to solve problems, to plan fun activities such as holidays and trips and to chat and 'check in' with one another. Children should be allowed have their say, express their needs and feelings, make their own suggestions and have a real input into the final agreements. Family meetings can be really important in helping children feel appreciated and supported and in giving them a sense of belonging. Overall, such meetings can help everyone stay connected and involved in each others lives and can bring the family closer together.

I HOPE SOMEDAY I'LL BE AS RESPONSIBLE A PARENT AS MY BIRTH PARENTS AND MY STEP PARENTS.

SOME USEFUL CONTACTS

IRELAND

AIM SERVICES
Family law information, family mediation, and counselling centre.
Address: 6 D'Olier Street, Dublin 2
Tel (01) 6708363
Monday to Friday 10.0 0am-1.00 pm
aimfamilyservices@eircom.net
www.aimfamilyservices.ie

AMEN
Men's support and advice line re domestic violence.
St Anne's Resource Centre,
Railway Street, Navan, Co. Meath
Tel (046) 9023718
info@amen.ie
www.amen.ie

FAMILY SUPPORT AGENCY MEDIATION SERVICE
Confidential service for people, married and non-married, who have decided to separate or divorce and who want to negotiate the terms of their separation or divorce with the help of a mediator. The agency have services and offices throughout the country.
First Floor, St Stephen's Green House,
Earlsfort Terrace, Dublin 2
Tel (01) 6344320
info@fsa.ie
www.fsa.ie.

FLAC (FREE LEGAL ADVICE CENTRES)
49 South William Street, Dublin 2
Tel (01) 679 4239
* do ask for solicitors who provide collaborative law services, which has the emphasis on helping couples resolve legal matters cooperatively and in a non-adversarial manner.

GINGERBREAD
Association for single, separated and sharing parents.
Carmichael House,
North Brunswick Street, Dublin 7
Tel (01) 8146618
info@gingerbread.ie
www.gingerbread.ie

LEGAL AID BOARD
For details of local legal aid centres. These provide civil legal aid, mainly in the area of family law, for people on low incomes. There is a scale of charges according to the means of the client.
Quay Street, Cahirciveen, Co. Kerry
Tel (066) 9471000 / 1890 615200
info@legalaidboard.ie
www.legalaidboard.ie

MOVE (MEN OVERCOMING VIOLENCE)
Supports the safety and wellbeing of women and their children who are experiencing violence or abuse through facilitating groups for violent men.
National Office, Unit 2, First Floor,
Clare Road Business Mall, Clare Road,
Ennis, County Clare
Tel (065) 6848689
move@moveireland.ie
www.moveireland.ie

MRCS
Marriage and Relationship Counselling Services for parents that are separated.
38 Upper Fitzwilliam Street, Dublin 2
Tel 1890 380 380
info@mrcs.ie
www.mrcs.ie

ONE FAMILY

Aims to affect positive change and achieve equality and social inclusion for all one-parent families in Ireland.

Cherish House,
2 Lower Pembroke Street, Dublin 2
Tel (01) 662 9212
info@onefamily.ie
www.onefamily.ie

ONE PARENT

Representing the views of local lone parent self-help groups nationwide.

Red Cow Lane, Smithfield, Dublin 7
Tel (01) 8148860
enquiries@oneparent.ie
www.oneparent.ie

PARENTAL EQUALITY

Working in support of shared parenting issues, promoting joint custody and equal social, tax, educational and welfare supports for both mothers and fathers.

15a Clanbrassil Street, Dundalk, Co. Louth
Tel (042) 9333163
www.parentalequality.ie.

PARENTLINE

Organisation and phoneline for parents under stress.

Carmichael House,
North Brunswick Street, Dublin 7
Tel (01) 8733500/1890 927 277
info@parentline.ie
www.parentline.ie

RAINBOWS

Facilitates groups to help children, teenagers, young adults and parents who have suffered loss through death, separation or divorce.

Rainbows National Office,
Loreto Centre, Crumlin Road, Dublin 12
Tel (01) 4734175
ask@rainbowsireland.com
www.rainbowsireland.com

ROLLERCOASTER

Provides practical advice on helping children through separation or divorce, dealing with legal and financial issues and on the challenges facing single parents. Chat forums are also available.

www.rollercoaster.ie

SHARED PARENTING IRELAND

Support group for single/separated parents who wish to continue parenting following relationship breakdown. Facilitates a father's family time afternoon.

Tel (087) 2939512
eolas@sharedparenting.org
www.sharedparenting.org

SOLO

Supports people parenting alone through the provision of a wide rang of information including family law, child education, and monetary matters.

Text (086) 2726429
info@solo.ie
www.solo.ie

TREOIR

Provides free information and referral services regarding pregnancy, counselling, social welfare, and legal rights.

14 Gandon House,
Custom House Square, IFSC, Dublin 1
Tel 1890 252 084
info@treoir.ie
www.treoir.ie

WOMEN'S AID

Provides support and information to women and their children who are being physically, emotionally and sexually abused in their own homes.

Everton House,
47 Old Cabra Road, Dublin 7
Tel 1800 341 900
info@womensaid.ie
www.womensaid.ie

When Parents Separate

UK

ACTION FOR CHILDREN-IT'S NOT YOUR FAULT
Practical information and mediation for children, young people and parents going through a family break-up
www.itsnotyourfault.org

DADS UK
A news and information site dedicated to giving a voice and support to all people interested in fathers' rights
http://dads-uk.co.uk

FAMILIES NEED FATHERS
Information, advice and support services keeping children and parents in contact on a national basis.
134 Curtain Road, London EC2A 3AR
Tel (0300) 0300 363
fnf@fnf.org.uk
www.fnf.org.uk

FAMILY MEDIATION BUREAU
Mediation and counselling for parents and children affected by separation.
Tel (0208) 315 7460
selondon.fmb@virgin.net
www.selondonfamilymediation.org.uk

GINGERBREAD
Championing the voices and needs of single parents and providing support services.
Helpline 0800 018 5026
www.gingerbread.org.uk

LEGAL SERVICES COMMISSION
Provides free information, advice and legal support for people on low incomes.
Tel (0845) 345 4345
www.legalservices.gov.uk

NATIONAL COUNCIL FOR ONE-PARENT FAMILIES
Standing up for single parents against poverty and prejudice.
255 Kentish Town Road,
London NW5 2LX
Tel 0800 018 5026
www.oneparentfamilies.org.uk

NATIONAL FAMILY MEDIATION
Helping parents reach joint decisions during separation.
Margaret Jackson Centre,
4 Barnfield Hill, Exeter, Devon EX1 1SR
Tel (01392) 271 610
general@nfm.org.uk
www.nfm.org.uk

PARENT LIFELINE
Emotional support and understanding for parents under stress.
Alpha House, 10-14 Carver Street,
Sheffield S1 4FS
Tel (0114) 272 6575
Web www.parentlifeline.org.uk

PARENTLINEPLUS
Incorporating Parentline, The National Stepfamily Association and Parent Network. Advice, information and support for parents and stepparents under stress.
520 High Gate Studios,
53-79 High Gate Road,
Kentish Town, London NW5 1TL
Tel (0207) 284 5500
parentsupport@parentlineplus.org.uk
www.parentlineplus.org.uk

SHARED PARENTING INFORMATION GROUP
Promoting responsible shared parenting after
separation and divorce. Includes information
on access centres, law reports and family
mediation.
www.spig.clara.net

WOMEN'S AID
Provides support and information to women
and their children who are being physically,
emotionally and sexually abused
Tel (0808) 2000 247
helpline@womensaid.org.uk
www.womensaid.org.uk

FURTHER READING/REFERENCES

Arbuthnot, J., & Gordon, D. A., *What About the Children: A Guide for Divorced and Divorcing Parents*, 4th edn (Ohio: The Center for Divorce Education, 1996)

Klatte, W. C., *Live-Away Dads* (New York: Penguin, 1999)

Ricci, I., *Mom's house, Dad's house* (New York: Fireside, 1997)

* The authors would like to acknowledge the influence of Arbuthnot & Gordon (1996) on the section entitled 'Helping Children Cope' and Klatte (1999) on 'Being a "Live-Away" Parent'.

OTHER BOOKS AND PROGRAMMES BY ATHORS

Sharry, J., & Fitzpatrick, C., *Parents Plus Children's Progamme: A video-based parenting guide to managing behaviour problems and promoting learning in children aged six to eleven* (Parents Plus Charity, c/o Mater Hospital, North Circular Road, Dublin 7, *www.parentsplus.ie*, 2007)

Sharry, J., Hampson, G., & Fanning, M., *Parenting preschoolers and young children: A practical guide to promoting confidence learning and good behaviour* (Dublin: Veritas Publications, 2005)

Sharry, J., *Positive Parenting: Bringing Up Responsible, Well-behaved and Happy Children* (Dublin: Veritas Publications, 2009)

Sharry, J., *Bringing Up Responsible Teenagers* (Dublin: Veritas Publications, 2001)

For further information and details of talks and seminars for parents see *www.solutiontalk.ie*